U.S. ENVIRONMENTAL PROTECTION AGENCY

OFFICE OF INSPECTOR GENERAL

Great Lakes National Program Should Improve Internal Controls to Ensure Effective Legacy Act Operations

Report No. 12-P-0407   April 9, 2012

Report Contributors:

Janet Kasper
Michael Petscavage
Wendy Swan
Nicole Pilate
Andres Calderon
Les Partridge

Abbreviations

CFC	Cincinnati Finance Center
EPA	U.S. Environmental Protection Agency
FAR	Federal Acquisition Regulation
FY	Fiscal year
GAO	U.S. Government Accountability Office
GLLA	Great Lakes Legacy Act of 2002
GLNPO	Great Lakes National Program Office
OIG	Office of Inspector General
OMB	Office of Management and Budget
RMDS	Resources Management Directives System
WAM	Work assignment manager

Cover photo: Equipment cleaning sediment at Kinnickinnic River site, Wisconsin. (EPA photo)

At a Glance

Why We Did This Review

We conducted this audit to determine whether the U.S. Environmental Protection Agency (EPA) has adequate controls over various financial aspects of the Great Lakes Legacy Act of 2002 (GLLA) funding and payments, and to determine whether project agreements contain goals that tie to the Agency's strategic plan, hold parties accountable, and ensure that nonfederal sponsors meet their obligations.

Background

Under GLLA, the Great Lakes National Program Office (GLNPO) performs sediment remediation using partnerships with nonfederal sponsors to accomplish the work. The nonfederal sponsor is required to provide a minimum of 35 percent of the effort in cash or in-kind contributions to the project.

For further information, contact our Office of Congressional and Public Affairs at (202) 566-2391.

The full report is at:
www.epa.gov/oig/reports/2012/20120409-12-P-0407.pdf

Great Lakes National Program Should Improve Internal Controls to Ensure Effective Legacy Act Operations

What We Found

GLLA program funding has increased five-fold over the last 7 years; however, the program has not established needed internal controls to ensure effective operations. For example, while GLLA project agreements contain environmental goals that tie to EPA's strategic plan:

- GLNPO is not timely forwarding project agreements to the EPA Finance Center.
- EPA is not tracking and recording actual in-kind contributions.
- GLLA project agreements do not always include exact due dates and amounts for payments from nonfederal sponsors.
- GLNPO has not been performing final accounting timely and does not keep adequate documentation of the reviews.
- GLNPO does not verify a nonfederal sponsor's financial capability or whether the nonfederal sponsor maintains an adequate accounting system prior to entering into a cost-sharing agreement.

Because of limited staffing at the beginning of the program, GLNPO's initial strategy was to focus on hiring essential technical staff (engineers and scientists) and leveraging the resources of other offices to help administer the program. The program has grown in terms of resources and staffing, but the focus on programmatic over financial activities negatively affected GLNPO's development of internal controls and led to many of the findings in this report. Without adequate internal controls, funds owed from nonfederal sponsors may not be collected timely, costs invoiced on GLLA projects may not be reasonable and allowable, and nonfederal sponsors with whom GLNPO enters into project agreements may not be able to meet their commitments.

What We Recommend

We recommend that EPA develop and implement policies and procedures for GLNPO that address the establishment of accounts receivable, recording of in-kind contributions, completion of final accounting, and reviews of the financial capability of nonfederal sponsors. EPA took action to address most of the recommendations and provided an action plan to address the remaining recommendation.

UNITED STATES ENVIRONMENTAL PROTECTION AGENCY
WASHINGTON, D.C. 20460

April 9, 2012

MEMORANDUM

SUBJECT: Great Lakes National Program Should Improve Internal Controls to
Ensure Effective Legacy Act Operations
Report No. 12-P-0407

FROM: Arthur A. Elkins, Jr.

TO: Susan Hedman
Regional Administrator, Region 5

Barbara J. Bennett
Chief Financial Officer

This is our report on the subject audit conducted by the Office of Inspector General (OIG) of the
U.S. Environmental Protection Agency. This report contains findings that describe the problems
the OIG has identified and corrective actions the OIG recommends.

The Region 5 and Great Lakes National Program Office staff are to be commended for the
prompt action that was taken to address the findings and recommendations as the issues were
identified during the audit.

Action Required

In responding to the draft report, the Agency provided a corrective action plan for addressing the
recommendations with milestone dates. Therefore, a response to the final report is not required.
The Agency should track corrective actions not implemented in the Management Audit Tracking
System. We have no objections to the further release of this report to the public. This report will
be available at http://www.epa.gov/oig.

If you or your staff have any questions regarding this report, please contact Melissa Heist,
Assistant Inspector General for Audit, at (202) 566-0899 or heist.melissa@epa.gov; or
Janet Kasper, Director for Contracts and Assistance Agreement Audits, at (312) 866-3059
or kasper.janet@epa.gov.

Table of Contents

Chapters

continued

Appendices

Chapter 1
Introduction

Purpose

The U.S. Environmental Protection Agency (EPA) Office of Inspector General (OIG) conducted this audit because of significant increases in Great Lakes Legacy Act of 2002 (GLLA) funding. Specifically, our audit objectives were to answer the following questions:

- Does EPA have adequate internal controls to (a) properly track and distribute GLLA funding, and (b) minimize improper payments?
- Do Great Lakes project agreements contain (a) goals and measures that further the goals in the Great Lakes and EPA strategic plans, and (b) mechanisms to hold parties accountable?
- Do the contracts that the Great Lakes National Program uses contain sufficient cost and schedule controls?
- Does EPA ensure that its nonfederal partners can meet their obligations to the Great Lakes National Program?

Background

Sediment contamination, primarily caused by industrialization in the Midwest, has been a problem in the Great Lakes for several decades. Historically, Great Lakes stakeholders have pursued sediment remediation through a variety of mechanisms, such as enforcement agreements and voluntary partnerships. It has been reported that polluted sediment is the largest major source of contaminants entering the food chain from Great Lakes rivers and harbors. This includes most of the areas of concern designated by the United States and Canada, the parties to the Great Lakes Water Quality Agreement. The Great Lakes Water Quality Agreement was first signed in 1972 and renewed in 1978. The agreement expresses the commitment of each country to restore and maintain the chemical, physical, and biological integrity of the Great Lakes Basin Ecosystem. EPA's Great Lakes National Program Office (GLNPO) was established in 1978 to oversee U.S. efforts to implement the Great Lakes Water Quality Agreement.

Congress passed GLLA to expedite the remediation of contaminated sediment sites and improve the ability of the United States to meet its commitments under the Great Lakes Water Quality Agreement. GLLA established an innovative approach to conducting sediment remediation in that it uses partnerships with nonfederal sponsors to accomplish the work. Project agreements under these partnerships require that the nonfederal sponsor provide a minimum of 35 percent of the effort in cash or in-kind contributions to the project.

With the exception of fiscal year (FY) 2010, GLLA funding from Congress has increased steadily since funding began in 2004 (table 1).

Table 1: GLLA funding

Fiscal year	Appropriated amount (in millions)
2004	$10
2005	22
2006	29
2007	30
2008	35
2009	37
2010	16
2011	50
Total	**$229**

Source: GLNPO.

When the program received its first GLLA funding in 2004, it had limited resources. In 2004, four GLNPO staff members were assigned to GLLA work. Eventually, GLNPO allocated more staff to GLLA work, and in 2011 approximately 12 staff members were performing GLLA work. Because of limited staffing at the beginning of the program, GLNPO's initial strategy was to focus on hiring essential technical staff (engineers and scientists) and to leverage the resources of other offices to help administer the program. For example, GLNPO did not award its own remediation contracts. Instead, it used existing Superfund remediation action contracts to perform GLLA work. GLNPO also did not hire financial staff and instead relied on its own technical staff to perform financial functions, and in some instances utilized a certified public accountant from the Region 5 Office of Counsel to perform required financial work.

As GLLA work has increased, leveraging resources of other offices has become more difficult and detrimental to those offices. For example, according to the acting director of GLNPO, GLLA projects began taking up too much capacity of the Superfund contracts being utilized, which could cause Superfund to procure new contracts more quickly as capacity runs out. The incongruent growth of GLNPO resources versus staffing, and the focus on programmatic over financial activities, had a major impact on GLNPO's development of internal controls and led to many of the issues we found in our audit.

Internal controls help government program managers achieve desired results through effective stewardship of public resources. Controls comprise the plans, methods, and procedures used to meet missions, goals, and objectives and, in doing so, support performance-based management. Managers are responsible for developing the detailed policies, procedures, and practices to fit their agencies' operations, and ensuring they are built into and are an integral part of operations. As programs change and as agencies strive to improve operational processes and implement new technological developments, management must continually assess and evaluate its internal controls to assure that they are effective and updated when necessary. The Government Accountability Office's (GAO's) *Standards for Internal Control in the Federal Government* state that management should ensure that skill needs are continually assessed and that the organization is able to obtain a workforce that has the required skills that match those necessary to meet organizational goals.

Noteworthy Achievements

Under GLLA, GLNPO has partnered with nonfederal sponsors to clean up areas of concern. As of February 2011, it reported completing remediation on 10 projects, resulting in the remediation of approximately 1,294,000 cubic yards of contaminated soil.

GLNPO expended approximately $175 million and has received approximately $121 million in nonfederal match. It has been successful in partnering with both state and local governments as well as 32 companies to complete these projects.

Scope and Methodology

We performed this audit from February 2011 to February 2012 in accordance with generally accepted government auditing standards, issued by the Comptroller General of the United States. Those standards require that we plan and perform the audit to obtain sufficient, appropriate evidence to provide a reasonable basis for our findings and conclusions based on our audit objectives. We believe that the evidence obtained provides a reasonable basis for our findings and conclusions based on our audit objectives.

During our audit, we examined information related to15 GLNPO projects (table 2).

Table 2: GLLA projects

1.	Black Lagoon
2.	Hog Island
3.	Ruddiman Creek
4.	Tannery Bay
5.	Kinnickinnic River
6.	Ashtabula River
7.	Ottawa River
8.	Grand Calumet River (West Branch/Roxana Marsh)
9.	St. Louis River
10.	St. Mary's River
11.	Lincoln Park
12.	Sheboygan River
13.	Division Street/Muskegon Lake
14.	Riverview, Detroit
15.	Waukegan Harbor

Source: GLNPO.

To determine whether EPA has adequate internal controls to properly track and distribute GLLA funding, we reviewed GLLA appropriations, determined the procedures GLNPO used for distributing and tracking funding, and tested key procedures related to the process. To determine whether GLNPO has adequate controls to minimize improper payments, we identified GLNPO procedures, tested the procedures to determine compliance, and interviewed GLNPO project officers.

With regard to whether Great Lakes project agreements contain (a) goals and measures that further the goals in the Great Lakes and EPA strategic plans, and (b) mechanisms to hold parties accountable, we reviewed the Great Lakes and EPA strategic plans. We also reviewed the project agreements and Office of Management and Budget (OMB) Circular A-11, and interviewed GLNPO management.

To examine whether the Great Lakes National Program uses contracts that contain sufficient cost and schedule controls, we reviewed current GLNPO contracts and examined the contract type of each contract. We also examined solicitations for contracts in process during our audit, and interviewed both GLNPO management and regional contracting officers regarding the structure of these new contracts.

To determine whether EPA ensures that its nonfederal partners can meet their obligations to the Great Lakes National Program, we reviewed the requirements of the project agreements. We interviewed GLNPO management and staff associated with performing final accounting procedures to determine the procedures performed and the associated documentation.

We reviewed documents EPA completed in compliance with the Federal Managers' Financial Integrity Act, including the Office of Administration and Resources Management's Fiscal Years 2010 and 2011 Federal Managers' Financial Integrity Act Assurance Letters. EPA did not identify internal control weaknesses directly related to our audit objectives.

Prior Audit Coverage

EPA OIG Report No. 09-P-0231, *EPA Needs a Cohesive Plan to Clean Up the Great Lakes Areas of Concern,* issued September 14, 2009; and EPA OIG Report No. 2006-P-00016, *EPA Can Better Implement Its Strategy for Managing Contaminated Sediments*, issued March 15, 2006, were the only previous audits relating to GLNPO. However, the recommendations cited in those reports were not relevant to the objectives of this audit.

Chapter 2
EPA Can Improve Internal Controls Over Great Lakes Legacy Act Payments

GLNPO project officers did not timely forward Legacy Act project agreements so that accounts receivable could be established, did not adequately document their reviews of contract invoices, and did not track or record in-kind contributions. EPA policies specify the procedures to ensure the timely recording of accounts receivable and the review of contractor invoices. GLNPO was unaware of existing accounts receivable and contract management policies, and EPA does not have a policy on accounting for in-kind contributions. When policies and procedures are either not in place or not followed, the risk of funds mismanagement, funds not being collected, or improper payments being made is increased.

GLNPO Did Not Timely Forward Project Agreements

Chapter 9 of EPA's Resources Management Directives System (RMDS) 2540-9-P1 requires program offices to forward legal agreements to the appropriate EPA finance center within 5 business days of an agreement's effective date. EPA's Cincinnati Finance Center (CFC) is responsible for preparing bills and receiving payments for nonjudicial accounts receivable. The finance center establishes the accounts receivable upon its receipt of the legal documents from EPA program offices. We found that GLNPO project officers did not timely forward to CFC the GLLA project agreements for any of the five projects we reviewed that required nonfederal sponsor cash payments on specific dates. As a result, CFC could not take actions, such as establishing and billing for accounts receivable, for $11,645,590 in cash payments required in the five project agreements (table 3).

Table 3: Project agreements requiring nonfederal sponsor cash payments not forwarded timely to CFC

Project agreement	Effective date	Date project agreement due to CFC	Date CFC received agreement	Number of days late to CFC	Total cash payment amounts
Hog Island	06/13/2005	06/20/2005	11/01/2006	499	$1,625,590
Tannery Bay	07/11/2006	07/18/2006	11/01/2006	106	2,620,000
Kinnickinnic River	07/14/2008	07/21/2008	01/13/2009	176	2,000,000
Lincoln Park	12/29/2010	01/05/2011	06/13/2011	159	5,000,000
Sheboygan River	12/29/2010	01/05/2011	01/13/2011	8	400,000
				Total	$11,645,590

Source: OIG analysis of EPA data.

The project agreements for the other 10 GLLA projects did not identify specific dates or amounts of cash contributions.

GLNPO project officers did not timely provide the project agreements to CFC because management was not aware of EPA's requirement to provide the signed project agreements to CFC within 5 business days of an agreement's effective date. Instead of providing the project agreements to CFC within 5 days of an agreement's effective date, GLNPO relied on its individual project managers to determine when billings to nonfederal sponsors should occur. When GLNPO project officers do not provide agreements to CFC timely, CFC cannot establish receivables timely, management does not have accurate data to make decisions, and collections of cash payments may be delayed. We found that for the 5 projects, EPA received all the collections from the nonfederal sponsors from 27 to 188 days after the due dates specified in the project agreements (table 4).

Table 4: Collections received for project agreements requiring nonfederal sponsor cash payments

Project name	Collection due date per agreement	Date collection received	Number of calendar days late	Cash amount
Hog Island	07/13/2005	09/26/2005	75	$719,500
	10/01/2005	12/19/2005	79	706,000
	10/01/2005	04/07/2006	188	200,090
Tannery Bay	08/11/2006	10/23/2006	73	460,000
	09/15/2006	11/15/2006	61	1,560,000
	12/06/2006[a]	01/02/2007	27	600,000
Kinnickinnic River	01/01/2009	02/10/2009	40	2,000,000
Lincoln Park	02/28/2010[b]	N/A	N/A	N/A
	03/01/2011	07/13/2011	134	5,000,000
Sheboygan River	01/03/2011	01/31/2011	28	100,000
	01/03/2011	02/18/2011	46	100,000
	01/03/2011	03/15/2011	71	100,000
	01/03/2011	03/21/2011	77	100,000
			Total	$11,645,590

Source: OIG analysis of EPA data.

Note: Reflects all amounts due for the 5 project agreements as of July 18, 2011.

[a] The project agreement required the nonfederal sponsor to make a $600,000 payment upon receipt of an invoice accompanied by documentation from GLNPO's contractor in an amount greater than or equal to $600,000. We determined that by November 6, 2006, EPA had paid contractor costs over $600,000; therefore, billings should have occurred by this date. We allowed 30 days for receipt of the collection in determining the number of days late.

[b] EPA/GLNPO did not invoice the nonfederal sponsor for the $190,000 specified in the agreement. When GLNPO sent the two Lincoln Park project agreements to CFC, the project officer told CFC not to bill the $190,000 because the amount was included in the $5 million.

Project Officers Do Not Document Contractor Invoice Reviews

GLNPO project officers act as the work assignment managers (WAMs) for GLLA projects and have primary responsibility for reviewing monthly contract invoices. Interim Policy Notice 10-04, Section 11.2 Revision of EPA's *Contracts Management Manual,* contains WAM responsibilities, procedures, and instructions for the processing of contract invoices (table 5). The manual requires WAMs to maintain documentation necessary to demonstrate that they conducted the invoice reviews and to note the elements of the invoices they reviewed.

Table 5: Work assignment manager responsibilities

Control feature	WAM level of responsibility
Monthly invoice reviews to verify: • Billed hours were worked by qualified personnel at the labor categories charged • Other direct costs are in accordance with contract requirements • Travel was accomplished and in accordance with contract requirements • Invoiced costs correlate to Monthly Progress Reports	Primary
Ensure quantities invoiced against delivery schedule and confirm receipt	Primary
Determine whether to suspend invoiced costs	Primary
Document the file, for example: • Ensure invoice contains sufficient explanation of billed costs • Maintain history of invoices submitted, payments accomplished, discounts taken, suspensions, disallowances, and refunds against the contract	Primary
Ensure subcontract costs are in accordance with contract requirements	Secondary

Source: EPA *Contracts Management Manual.*

The Interim Policy Notice provides a checklist to assist WAMs with their invoice reviews, and states that use of the checklist constitutes adequate file documentation in support of a complete and comprehensive invoice review. When the checklist is not used, the policy requires additional documentation be maintained. According to the interim policy, if the project officer, or work assignment manager, elects not to use the checklist, then other documentation, such as spreadsheets, tabulations, notes, etc., must be used to demonstrate that invoices were properly reviewed, noting what was reviewed on each invoice.

Upon completion of invoice reviews, the Interim Policy Notice instructs WAMs to provide the Superfund project officer with written invoice approval, either via the checklist or other documentation. All eight WAMs that we interviewed reported performing the required invoice reviews. However, those WAMs did not use the invoice review checklist or maintain the type of documentation required to demonstrate that invoices were properly reviewed. Instead of using the checklist, WAMs used the two-way memo created by EPA to document a WAM's review and payment approval of a monthly invoice. While EPA's two-way memo does document a WAM's review and approval of an invoice, it does not provide the required support or serve as adequate file documentation of what and how the invoice was reviewed. Further, three of the eight WAMs interviewed did not always send EPA's two-way memo that certified their invoice review and payment approval to the Superfund project officer. One of the three WAMs stated that although he was in agreement with all of the invoices, he did not provide a formal e-mail approval to the Superfund project officer.

The WAMs were unaware of the Interim Policy Notice's requirement to maintain documentary evidence to support their monthly invoice reviews and to approve each payment. Some WAMs had not received the contract officer representative training in several years. GLNPO did not have any procedures to ensure or verify that WAMs were performing adequate invoice reviews, approving the payments, or maintaining the required support for the invoice reviews. The growth and development of the GLNPO program, as described in the report background, contributed to the lack of procedures.

When WAMs do not adequately document their invoice reviews or submit the required payment approvals, EPA has limited assurance that the costs invoiced on the GLLA projects are reasonable and allowable. In addition, management cannot determine the adequacy of the reviews performed.

EPA Does Not Record or Track GLLA In-Kind Contributions

EPA does not have a policy to address the recording of in-kind services nonfederal sponsors provide. GAO's *Standards for Internal Control in the Federal Government* require that (1) transactions be promptly recorded to maintain their relevance and value to management in controlling operations and making decisions; and (2) transactions and other significant events be clearly documented, with the documentation readily available for examination. In-kind services represent a financial transaction that should be recorded in EPA's accounting system.

EPA does not track or record the in-kind contributions it receives from GLLA nonfederal sponsors in its accounting system because it does not have associated policies and procedures. The nonfederal sponsors typically provide in-kind services such as construction oversight, materials, design or engineering services, payroll, travel costs, and laboratory services. GLNPO does maintain a spreadsheet that incorporates nonfederal sponsor costs along with the EPA costs incurred for each project.

If the accounting system does not reflect the total cost of the program, EPA management may make decisions or projections based on information that is not accurate or complete. In addition, EPA may not report the total costs of projects accurately or timely. The actual and estimated in-kind contributions for the 15 GLLA projects examined are significant, totaling $96 million of the total $121 million in nonfederal sponsor costs for the projects (table 6).

Table 6: Actual and estimated in-kind contribution by project

Project name	Nonfederal sponsor's share of project costs	Potential in-kind contributions	Actual/ estimated
Black Lagoon	$3,111,131	$3,111,131	Actual
Hog Island	2,205,000	579,410	Estimated
Ruddiman Creek	4,939,436	593,641	Actual
Tannery Bay	3,261,033	641,033	Actual
Kinnickinnic River	8,400,000	6,400,000	Estimated
Ashtabula River	30,500,000	30,500,000	Estimated
Ottawa River	24,500,000	24,500,000	Estimated
St. Louis River	1,500,000	1,500,000	Estimated
St. Mary's River	1,600,000	1,600,000	Estimated
Lincoln Park	8,610,000	2,110,000	Estimated
Sheboygan River	400,000	[a]0	Estimated
Division Street/Muskegon Lake	4,200,000	4,200,000	Estimated
Riverview, Detroit	175,000	130,509	Estimated
Waukegan Harbor	140,000	77,432	Estimated
Grand Calumet River (West Branch/Roxana Marsh)[b]	27,833,750	19,923,750	Estimated
Total	$121,375,350	$95,866,906	

Source: OIG analysis of EPA data.

[a] The nonfederal sponsor's share of the remedial action for Sheboygan River will be 100 percent in-kind contributions. Because remedial action work will not begin until 2012, the potential dollar amount is unknown at this time.
[b] The GLNPO project agreement does not specify the amounts to be received as in-kind and cash. The potential amounts represent the unpaid portion of the nonfederal sponsor's share.

The projects with actual in-kind contributions listed in table 6 represent closed Legacy Act projects for which GLNPO has verified the total costs of the projects and the nonfederal sponsors' in-kind contributions. Projects containing estimated amounts for in-kind contributions are ongoing. Therefore, the in-kind contributions represent the potential amount GLNPO may receive from the nonfederal sponsors. The estimated contributions take into account the total nonfederal sponsor cost share for the project, which is documented in the project agreements, and any cash payments previously made by the nonfederal sponsors.

Recommendations

We recommend that the Regional Administrator, Region 5, direct the Director of GLNPO to:

1. Establish a procedure to forward signed GLLA project agreements to CFC within 5 days of an agreement's effective date as required by RMDS 2540, Chapter 9, and notify project officers of the procedure.

2. Implement a procedure for holding project officers accountable for the WAM's responsibilities regarding the invoice review process specified in EPA's *Contract Management Manual*.

We recommend that the Chief Financial Officer, in coordination with the Director of GLNPO:

3. Develop and implement policies and procedures to consistently record and track in-kind contributions from private- and public-sector nonfederal sponsors for all GLLA projects.

Agency Response and OIG Evaluation

In response to recommendations 1 and 2, GLNPO developed two operating procedures:

- *Review and Acceptance of Both Monetary and In-Kind Match Contributions by Non federal Sponsors (NFS) under the Great Lakes Legacy Act*
- *Review, Acceptance, and Documentation of Task Order and Work Assignment Monthly Progress Reports and Invoices by GLNPO CORs*

The revised operating procedures address the finding and recommendations.

In response to recommendation 3, the Office of the Chief Financial Officer will convene an Agency workgroup to develop and implement policies and procedures to consistently record and track in-kind contributions from private- and public-sector nonfederal sponsors for all GLLA projects. These policies and procedures will be completed by December 31, 2012. The Agency's actions, when implemented, will address the recommendation.

Chapter 3
Project Agreements Can Be Improved to Increase Accountability

Although GLLA project agreements have goals and measures to further the Great Lakes and EPA strategic plan goals, GLLA project agreements do not always include payment dates, and project officers do not ensure that nonfederal sponsors submit required progress reports. Management is responsible for developing policies, procedures, and practices to ensure that internal controls are built into their operations. As the GLLA program developed, GLNPO focused on the technical aspects of projects more than it did on administrative responsibilities. Without additional internal controls to increase accountability, the Agency is vulnerable to not receiving required cost-share payments and not being able to support its reported performance.

GLLA Projects Align With EPA Strategic Plan Goals

GLLA projects further EPA's goal to remediate a cumulative total of 8 million cubic yards of contaminated sediment in the Great Lakes. GLLA project agreements contain goals and measures (e.g., sediment removal amounts) that tie to EPA's strategic plan, and GLNPO has instituted a pre-project-approval process that ensures that each GLLA project furthers EPA's strategic plan. We sampled five project files, and all five contained pre-project-agreement documents that illustrated GLNPO's efforts to ensure that each project would reduce risks to human health and restore the Great Lakes ecosystem. GLNPO has established a technical review committee to review each proposed project to ensure that selected projects reduce risks to human health and restore the ecosystem by reducing contaminated sediments.

Project Agreements Are Missing Payment Dates

When cash payments were anticipated, GLNPO did not always include a payment due date or amounts of the cash payments in the project agreements. Of the 15 GLLA projects we examined, the agreements for 10 projects did not contain cash payment amounts or due dates. However, 3 of the 10 projects have received cash payments from the nonfederal sponsor. These three project agreement's payment terms were not specific enough to allow for accounts receivable to be established. For example:

- The project agreement for Grand Calumet River (West Branch/Roxana Marsh) calls for periodic billings, with no indication of how much of the 35 percent match ($27.8 million) is expected to be cash versus in-kind contributions. The project officer periodically reviews how much money the contractor has expended and how much is left to be expended to determine when more money is needed from the nonfederal sponsor. The project officer asserted that the majority of the match would be cash contributions, and approximately $7.4 million has been received to date.

All GLLA projects have a 35 percent match requirement from the nonfederal sponsor, which can be cash or in-kind services. EPA RMDS 2540-9-P1, Billing and Collecting, states that a receivable should be recognized when a federal entity establishes a claim to cash or other assets against other entities, either based on legal provisions, such as a payment due date, or goods or services provided. If the exact amount is unknown, a reasonable estimate is to be made.

GLNPO management stated that the program modeled GLLA project agreements after U.S. Army Corps of Engineers project agreements. However, the GLLA project agreements are not consistently modeled on those of the Corps, as the Corps model project agreement shows a required monetary contribution and options for the timing of the sponsor's payment, and some of the GLLA project agreements do not.

Without a reasonable estimate of the amount of cash payments and their due dates, the finance center cannot automatically initiate the accounts receivable process; the finance center must rely on the GLLA project officers to notify it that cash payments are due. Without accurate accounts receivable, nonfederal sponsor cost shares may not be received, which could signify that the nonfederal sponsor cannot meet its cost share obligation. According to the Region 5 Office of Regional Counsel, if the nonfederal sponsor cost share is not received, work on the project in question would stop, potentially decreasing public health benefits and wasting federal funds.

GLNPO Is Not Receiving Required Progress Reports

Project officers do not always receive required progress reports from the nonfederal sponsors. Of the 11 project agreements we sampled for progress reports, 6 required the nonfederal sponsor to submit quarterly or periodic progress reports. However, for all six of these projects, none of the project officers collected written progress reports from the nonfederal sponsor.

The progress report requirements included in each project agreement vary for each project. The requirements range from a general requirement for a report with no details of what the report should include, to requirements that specify inclusion of a summary of work, a current schedule of work and milestones, a discussion of costs incurred to date, and the percentage of the nonfederal sponsor's costs paid to date. Regardless of the level of detail specified in project agreements, the respective project officers asserted that they frequently received oral reports from the nonfederal sponsors and therefore did not require written progress reports.

This project officer practice creates an environment of limited access to project data. When the project officer is unavailable, orally reported project data are also unavailable, and continued monitoring in the absence of the project officer may be difficult. The Agency also potentially misses an opportunity to improve efficiencies and prevent waste when historical project progress data are not obtained and stored.

Recommendation

We recommend that the Regional Administrator, Region 5, direct the Director of GLNPO to:

4. Develop and implement policies and procedures that will result in consistent project agreements with improved accountability. The policies and procedures should address:

   a. Inclusion of specific payment due dates.
   b. Collection of written nonfederal sponsor status reports at least quarterly.

Agency Response and OIG Evaluation

To address the recommendation, EPA developed a new model project agreement. The revisions to the project agreement addressed the finding and recommendation.

Chapter 4
GLNPO Has Improved Contract Cost Controls

GLNPO has awarded new contracts that will allow it to increase competition and fixed-price contracting. The Federal Acquisition Regulation (FAR) notes that the government incurs additional cost risks and takes on the additional burden of managing the contractor's costs in cost-reimbursement contracts. Further, in 2009, OMB and the President issued documents encouraging federal entities to utilize more fixed-price contracting and competition. As GLNPO began the process of awarding its own contracts, it decided, in coordination with Region 5's contracting office, to use a contract type and structure that would increase competition and the use of fixed-price task orders. These new GLNPO contracts incentivize contractors to control costs and perform effectively, and minimize GLNPO's own administrative burden.

Fixed-Price Contracts Help Programs Control Costs and Perform Efficiently

According to the FAR, when the government selects a cost-reimbursement contract, the government incurs additional cost risks and takes on the additional burden of managing the contractor's costs. The FAR notes that past experience provides a basis for firmer pricing, and contracting officers should avoid protracted use of cost-reimbursement or time-and-materials contracts. The FAR also suggests that contracting officers should consider whether a portion of the contract can be established on a firm-fixed-price basis if the entire contract cannot be firm-fixed-price.

Bolstering the FAR's message, the March 2009 Presidential memorandum states that excessive reliance by executive agencies on sole-source contracts (or contracts with a limited number of sources) and cost-reimbursement contracts creates a risk that taxpayer funds will be spent on contracts that are wasteful, inefficient, subject to misuse, or otherwise not well designed to serve the needs of the federal government or the interests of the American taxpayer. The memorandum states that there shall be a preference for fixed-price-type contracts. The October 2009 OMB memorandum, *Increasing Competition and Structuring Contracts for the Best Results*, stresses that fixed-price contracts provide greater incentive than cost-reimbursement contracts for the contractor to control costs and perform efficiently, and that Agencies should examine their use of noncompetitive contracts. Noncompetitive contracts place agencies in the position of having to negotiate contracts without the benefit of a direct market mechanism to help establish pricing. Further, a December 2009 OMB document, *Saving Money and Improving Government*, warns that cost-reimbursement and time-and-materials contracts provide limited incentive for the contractor to control costs and maximize value.

GLNPO Is Increasing Competition and Fixed-Price Contracting

GLNPO has historically used existing level-of-effort, cost-reimbursement Superfund contracts to accomplish its work. However, as GLNPO has grown over the years, it became necessary to award its own contracts to accomplish the work. GLNPO awarded three new contracts for construction in August and September 2011. These contracts are indefinite delivery/indefinite quantity; however, GLNPO plans to issue mostly fixed-price task orders under these contracts. The contracting officer stated that he plans to document the contract file each time a task order other than fixed-price is awarded. However, there currently are no procedures in place to ensure that the contracting officer documents the rationale for not using fixed-price task orders. GLNPO plans to compete future task orders among the three construction contractors. This increased competition will help ensure that GLNPO receives a fair and reasonable price for the services.

By instituting fixed-price components in its contracts, GLNPO is using contracts that contain better cost and schedule controls that reduce risk to the government. According to the Federal Acquisition Regulations, firm-fixed-price task orders provide for a price that is not subject to adjustment on the basis of the contractor's cost experience in performing the contract. This contract type places upon the contractor maximum risk and full responsibility for all costs and resulting profit or loss. It provides maximum incentive for the contractor to control costs and perform effectively, and imposes a minimum administrative burden upon the contracting parties. Additionally, GLNPO's decision to compete task orders allows it to realize direct market benefits in establishing the task order price.

Recommendation

We recommend that the Regional Administrator, Region 5, direct the Acquisition and Assistance Branch Chief to:

5. Implement procedures to monitor and ensure that the rationale for not using fixed-price task orders under the new GLNPO contracts is documented.

Agency Response and OIG Evaluation

In response to the recommendation, the Region 5 Acquisition Section will use fixed-price task orders to the fullest extent possible. There may be certain circumstances where fixed-price task orders are not appropriate. Task orders that cannot be awarded on a fixed-price basis will be thoroughly documented, with input from GLNPO, by the Acquisition Staff before the task order is issued. The Contracting Officer will be responsible for this determination. The Agency's action addressed the recommendation.

Chapter 5
EPA Should Develop Internal Controls to Better Ensure Its Nonfederal Sponsors Meet Their Obligations

GLNPO has not timely completed the final accountings required for GLLA projects, does not keep evidence supporting procedures performed and rationale for allowed and disallowed costs, does not verify the financial capability of the nonfederal sponsor prior to entering into an agreement, and does not verify that the nonfederal sponsor has an adequate accounting system. GAO's *Standards for Internal Control in the Federal Government* require management to develop policies and procedures that lead to effective and efficient management of agency programs. GLNPO does not have policies and procedures regarding the timing of, procedures for, or documentation of final accounting; determining the financial capability of the nonfederal sponsors; or verifying the adequacy of nonfederal sponsor accounting systems. In the absence of policies and procedures, management has limited assurance that the costs submitted by nonfederal sponsors are reasonable and allowable.

Internal Controls Are Required

GAO's *Standards for Internal Control in the Federal Government* states that management is responsible for developing the detailed policies, procedures, and practices to fit agency operations, and ensuring that the policies, procedures, and practices are an integral part of operations. GLLA project agreements require that a final accounting be performed at the end of each project to ensure that the nonfederal sponsor has contributed its cost share in accordance with the project agreement. Additionally, the GLLA project agreements require the nonfederal sponsor to have an adequate accounting system. Without an accounting system that tracks cost by project and by individual cost element, nonfederal costs applicable to the project cannot be verified during the final accounting.

GLNPO Should Improve Final Accounting

GLNPO has completed only 3 final accountings for the 10 projects reported as complete. Some have taken over 4 ½ years from the time of final payment on the project to the date the final accounting was completed (table 7).

Table 7: Projects completed with a final accounting

Project	Project end date	Last payment date	Date of final accounting	Months from project end to final accounting	Months from last payment to final accounting
Black Lagoon	November 2005	07/20/2006	03/11/2011	5 yrs., 4 mos.	4 yrs., 8 mos.
Ruddiman Creek	May 2006	08/23/2006	03/29/2011	4 yrs., 10 mos.	4 yrs., 7 mos.
Tannery Bay	August 2007	06/04/2008	10/30/ 2008	1 yr., 2 mos.	4 mos.
			Average	3 yrs., 9 mos.	3 yrs., 2 mos.

Source: OIG analysis of EPA data.

In addition to the three completed final accountings, there are two other projects that GLNPO has listed as complete for which no payments have been made in over a year, and the final accounting has not been completed (table 8). Even though GLNPO considers five more projects as complete, the projects either have small amounts of work to be performed or have costs that need to be finalized before the final accounting can take place.

Table 8: Completed projects with no final accounting

Project	Project end date	Last payment date	Months from project end to August 2011	Months from last payment to August 2011
Hog Island	November 2006	03/04/2009	4 yrs., 9 mos.	2 yrs., 5 mos.
St. Louis River	December 2010	06/14/2010	8 mos.	1 yr., 2 mos.

Source: OIG analysis of EPA data.

GLNPO is not adequately documenting the procedures performed during the final accounting, nor is it documenting the basis for disallowing or allowing costs submitted by the nonfederal sponsor. For the three completed final accounting, there was no documentation of what costs were reviewed, how the costs were reviewed, and why costs were allowed or disallowed. For example, there was no evidence that indirect rates were reviewed or verified. The GLNPO staff member performing the final accounting told us that he did not verify the indirect rates. Based on the records kept, an independent third party would have difficulty determining what procedures were performed and whether those procedures were adequate.

GLNPO Is Not Verifying Financial Capability or Accounting System Adequacy

GLNPO is not verifying that the nonfederal sponsor has the financial capability to meet project agreement obligations or the ability to account for, track, and report project costs. Nonfederal sponsors agree to provide millions of dollars of in-kind services and cash as part of a GLLA cost-sharing agreement. Thus, before entering into an agreement, it would be prudent for EPA to verify that the nonfederal sponsor had the financial resources to meet its obligations in the project agreement. Additionally, it would be prudent to verify in advance whether the nonfederal sponsor maintains an accounting system that tracks and reports costs by project. GLNPO did not perform financial capability reviews and did not verify that the nonfederal sponsor maintained an adequate accounting system that could report costs by project. Discussions with GLNPO management confirmed that these reviews were not performed.

Lack of Policies and Procedures Leave GLNPO Vulnerable

GLNPO has not emphasized the completion and documentation of final accounting. This is largely because the program began with limited resources, and management was unsure about the longevity of the program. Therefore, in making decisions regarding policies and procedures and staffing, management concentrated on programmatic mission issues instead of financial and administrative tasks. As a result, GLNPO does not have policies and procedures regarding the timing of final accounting or the procedures to be performed and documentation to be retained. Without adequate policies and procedures, management cannot meet its goals for accountability and effective and efficient use of resources. Management also has limited assurance that the nonfederal sponsors have met the cost share for the completed projects. Additionally, because the final accounting was not being done timely, GLNPO and EPA risk that documentation may be lost or that EPA or nonfederal sponsor staff with institutional knowledge of the projects and costs incurred may leave, which would make completion of the final accounting difficult.

Additionally, the final accounting is not being completed timely because GLNPO does not verify actual in-kind contributions or request the source documentation to support the in-kind contributions from nonfederal sponsors until after the completion of GLLA projects. GLNPO management noted that it was sometimes an "arduous" task to review the many boxes of invoices and determine the value of the in-kind services. One project officer reported receiving thousands of documents after completion of a project. Requesting and receiving documentation on an interim basis could improve the overall final accounting process.

GLNPO also does not have policies and procedures for verifying the financial capability and accounting system adequacy of nonfederal sponsors. Without verifying the financial capability, GLNPO is entering into project agreements without reasonable assurance that the nonfederal sponsor can meet the commitments. Moreover, by not verifying the adequacy of the nonfederal sponsor's accounting system, GLNPO is vulnerable to fraud, waste, and abuse in that it does not have reasonable assurance that costs submitted as in-kind costs are associated with the project and are reasonable and allowable.

Recommendations

We recommend that the Regional Administrator, Region 5, direct the Director of GLNPO to:

6. Develop and implement policies and procedures on how to complete final accounting of project costs and when the final accounting is to be completed.

7. Develop and implement policies and procedures to review nonfederal sponsor in-kind costs on a periodic basis during the project.

8. Develop and implement policies and procedures to verify the financial capability of nonfederal sponsors and the adequacy of nonfederal sponsor accounting systems prior to entering into project agreements.

Agency Response and OIG Evaluation

In response to recommendations 6 and 7, GLNPO developed two standard operating procedures:

- *Great Lakes Legacy Act (GLLA) Project Agreement (PA) Closeout*
- *Review and Acceptance of Both Monetary and In-Kind Match Contributions by Nonfederal Sponsors (NFS) Under the Great Lakes Legacy Act*

In response to recommendation 8, GLNPO modified its project agreement to include specific language that addresses certification of financial capability, audit requirements, and recordkeeping.

The procedures and revised project agreement address the findings and recommendations.

Status of Recommendations and Potential Monetary Benefits

<table>
<tr><th colspan="6">RECOMMENDATIONS</th><th colspan="2">POTENTIAL MONETARY BENEFITS (in $000s)</th></tr>
<tr><th>Rec. No.</th><th>Page No.</th><th>Subject</th><th>Status[1]</th><th>Action Official</th><th>Planned Completion Date</th><th>Claimed Amount</th><th>Agreed-To Amount</th></tr>
<tr><td>1</td><td>11</td><td>Direct the Director of GLNPO to establish a procedure to forward signed GLLA project agreements to CFC within 5 days of an agreement's effective date as required by RMDS 2540, Chapter 9, and notify project officers of the procedure.</td><td>C</td><td>Regional Administrator, Region 5</td><td>3/8/2012</td><td></td><td></td></tr>
<tr><td>2</td><td>11</td><td>Direct the Director of GLNPO to implement a procedure for holding project officers accountable for the WAM's responsibilities regarding the invoice review process specified in EPA's *Contract Management Manual*.</td><td>C</td><td>Regional Administrator, Region 5</td><td>3/8/2012</td><td></td><td></td></tr>
<tr><td>3</td><td>11</td><td>Coordinate with the Director of GLNPO to develop and implement policies and procedures to consistently record and track in-kind contributions from private- and public-sector nonfederal sponsors for all GLLA projects.</td><td>O</td><td>Chief Financial Officer</td><td>12/30/2012</td><td></td><td></td></tr>
<tr><td>4</td><td>14</td><td>Direct the Director of GLNPO to develop and implement policies and procedures that will result in consistent project agreements with improved accountability. The policies and procedures should address:

a. Inclusion of specific payment due dates.

b. Collection of written nonfederal sponsor status reports at least quarterly.</td><td>C</td><td>Regional Administrator, Region 5</td><td>3/8/2012</td><td></td><td></td></tr>
<tr><td>5</td><td>16</td><td>Direct the Acquisition and Assistance Branch Chief to implement procedures to monitor and ensure that the rationale for not using fixed-price task orders under the new GLNPO contracts is documented.</td><td>C</td><td>Regional Administrator, Region 5</td><td>3/8/2012</td><td></td><td></td></tr>
<tr><td>6</td><td>20</td><td>Direct the Director of GLNPO to develop and implement policies and procedures on how to complete final accounting of project costs and when the final accounting is to be completed.</td><td>C</td><td>Regional Administrator, Region 5</td><td>3/8/2012</td><td></td><td></td></tr>
<tr><td>7</td><td>20</td><td>Direct the Director of GLNPO to develop and implement policies and procedures to review nonfederal sponsor in-kind costs on a periodic basis during the project.</td><td>C</td><td>Regional Administrator, Region 5</td><td>3/8/2012</td><td></td><td></td></tr>
<tr><td>8</td><td>20</td><td>Direct the Director of GLNPO to develop and implement policies and procedures to verify the financial capability of nonfederal sponsors and the adequacy of nonfederal partner accounting systems prior to entering into project agreements.</td><td>C</td><td>Regional Administrator, Region 5</td><td>3/8/2012</td><td></td><td></td></tr>
</table>

O = recommendation is open with agreed-to corrective actions pending
C = recommendation is closed with all agreed-to actions completed
U = recommendation is unresolved with resolution efforts in progress

Agency Response

March 8, 2012

MEMORANDUM

SUBJECT: Response of the Great Lakes National Program Office (GLNPO) to Office
Of Inspector General (OIG) Draft Audit Report: Great Lakes National
Program Should Improve Internal Controls to Ensure Effective Legacy
Act Operations; Project No. OA-FY11-O153

FROM: Susan Hedman
Great Lakes National Program Manager

TO: Melissa M. Heist
Assistant Inspector General for Audit

We have reviewed your February 9, 2012 Draft Audit Report that included findings and
recommendations concerning the Great Lakes Legacy Act program. Concurrent with the
initiation of the OIG audit, GLNPO began the process of establishing Standard Operating
Procedures and other mechanisms to address the types of issues identified in your draft report.
Our discussions with OIG staff in connection with your audit helped us to complete and
implement these new procedures, starting in the fall of 2011.

Specifically:

We have finalized and implemented SOPs to address Recommendations 1, 2, 6, and 7 in the
February 9th Draft Audit Report:

> SOP to Address Recommendation 1: *Review and Acceptance of Both Monetary
> and In-Kind Match Contributions by Non federal Sponsors (NFS) under the Great
> Lakes Legacy Act,*
>
> SOP to Address Recommendation 2: *Review, Acceptance, and Documentation of
> Task Order and Work Assignment Monthly Progress Reports and Invoices by
> GLNPO CORs.*
>
> SOP to Address Recommendation 6: *Great Lakes Legacy Act (GLLA) Project
> Agreement (PA) Closeout.*
>
> SOP to Address Recommendation 7: Review and Acceptance of Both Monetary
> and In-Kind Match Contributions by Nonfederal Sponsors (NFS) Under the Great
> Lakes Legacy Act.

With respect to **Recommendation 5** in the Report, please note that, in 2011, three new remediation contracts were awarded for Great Lakes Legacy Act projects, utilizing fixed-price features. The Region 5 Acquisition Section will use fixed-price task orders to the fullest extent possible. There may be certain circumstances where fixed-price task orders are not appropriate. Task orders that cannot be awarded on a fixed-price basis will be thoroughly documented, with input from GLNPO, by the Acquisition Staff before the task order is issued. The Contracting Officer will be responsible for this determination.

With respect to **Recommendations 4 and 8**, a new model project agreement was completed and will be utilized for all new projects. The new model project agreement adds very specific language that addresses certification of financial capability, audit requirements, and recordkeeping.

Finally, with respect to **Recommendation 3**, I note that in April, OCFO's Office of Financial Management will convene an agency workgroup with the Office of Financial Services, Region 5 and the Interagency Agreement Shared Service Center to develop and implement policies and procedures to consistently record and track in-kind contributions from private- and public-sector nonfederal sponsors for all GLLA projects. These policies and procedures will be completed by December 31, 2012.

Again, my thanks to you and your staff for the assistance you provided. Any questions regarding this response can be directed to Chris Korleski, Great Lakes National Program Office Director, at 312-353-4891, or to me at 312-886-3000.

cc: Cameron Davis, Senior Advisor to the Administrator
        Chris Korleski, Director, Great Lakes National Program Office
        Tinka Hyde, Director, Water Division, U.S. EPA Region 5
        Robert A. Kaplan, Regional Counsel, U.S. EPA Region 5
        Eric Levy, Region 5 Audit Coordinator

Distribution

Office of the Administrator
Assistant Administrator for Water
Regional Administrator, Region 5
Agency Follow-Up Official (the CFO)
Agency Follow-Up Coordinator
General Counsel
Associate Administrator for Congressional and Intergovernmental Relations
Associate Administrator for External Affairs and Environmental Education
Director, Office of Acquisition Management, Office of Administration and Resources
      Management
Audit Follow-Up Coordinator, Office of the Chief Financial Officer
Audit Follow-Up Coordinator, Region 5
Public Affairs Officer, Region 5
Director, Great Lakes National Program Office